Splinters of Glass

Written by
Arleen Watson

Compiled and Edited by
Donna Watson

Foreword by Serena Dyer

Soul Attitude Press

Copyright © 2016 by Donna Watson
All rights reserved.

No part of this book may be reproduced or transmitted in any form or by any means, electronic or mechanical, including photocopying, recording or by any information storage and retrieval system, without permission in writing from the copyright holder.

Published by Soul Attitude Press
Pinellas Park, FL

ISBN: 978-1-939181-79-4

Printed in the United States of America

For
Nancy and Donna
Beloved daughters
Never give up!

ARW

I was always trying for the prize!
I would seem about to attain it
But as I went to grasp it
The sparkling crystal would break
And I would be left
Clutching only "Splinters of Glass."

Table of Contents

Foreword vii

Introduction 1

I. Loneliness
    Advice to the Lonely 9
    The Rain Barrel 11
    Summer Wind 13
    The Drought 15
    Pinnacles 17

II. Travels
    New York 21
    New York Again! 23
    Nassau 25
    Rocks in the Sun (Nassau) 27
    Reunion 29

III. Scars of the Heart
    The Little Scar 33
    The House 35
    For Those Who Come 37
    Birth of Joy 39
    War 41
    New Generation 43
    The Little Ones 45

IV. Bitter Harvest
    Survival 49
    Sick-abed 51
    Pain 53
    The Puzzle 55
    The Thirst 57
    Affair at End 59
    Rhapsody 61

    The Foolish Heart 63
    To a Woman Very Dear 65

V. The Family
    Donna – Flight 69
    Donna – The Road 71
    The Little Brown Seal (Donna) 73
    Nancy 75
    My Sister – The Visit 77
    Mother 79
    My Husband 81

VI. Pebbles
    The Doe 85
    Death Dances Too 87
    The Loner 89
    Thoughts 91
    The Shopper 95
    The Summit 97

VII. Memories
    Memories 101
    In Memory 103
    The Party 105
    Blue Midnight 107
    The Outsider 109

VIII. The Men
    Al Jolson 113
    I Am So Free 115
    My Doctor 117
    Dr. Jack Greener 119
    Piper Pan 121

    About the Author 123

Foreword

I believe that when we are born we arrive with a certain dharma or purpose, if you will. Some are born to sing, or paint, to teach or to study law. For me, I was born into a family of writers and a legacy of expanded forward thinking minds. I was blessed to have the opportunity to grow up with and study with some of our greatest spiritual visionaries and teachers of spiritual wisdom.

Though I appreciate all types of literature, I have a personal affinity for good poetry. Good in the sense that when words paint vivid pictures in your mind with vibrancy and causes emotional peaks that make you feel the author's strife or struggle or triumph in your heart.

Knowing my fondness for unusual and profound poetry, a family friend shared with us Splinters of Glass written by her mother over thirty years ago. As I began to read one poem, then another, and yet another, which made me feel the heart of Arleen, I wanted to know more about the author. Arleen was a woman born with passages of birth that could have confined her to a life of sullenness and surrender. She was bipolar and lived in a time that didn't recognize or understand the disease. She was also born beautiful and talented, and she enjoyed an unabashed love of men and sex that her generation didn't talk about, let alone write about. She authored many poems under the pseudonym of Pan Anderson so she could write freely but anonymously.

My father, Wayne Dyer, read many of her poems before he died and was moved by the authenticity and passion that Arleen wrote with. We often say people wear their heart on their sleeves. Arleen wore her heart like a badge of courage pinned front and center on her chest.

I am sorry she passed before I could meet her, but when I finished reading her poems I felt like I knew her once upon a time.

I invite all of you to take a walk on a beautiful day in the park, or curl up next to a lit fire and bring Arleen's words with you, as you will find her good company. Splinters of Glass, a treasure chest full of greatness.

Serena Dyer

Introduction

When I sat down to write the introduction to my mother's book, I felt a heavy responsibility to properly and without prejudice talk about a woman who is well worth reading about and whose poetry is well worth reciting. Sharing what she was able to accomplish in her life with so many strikes against her is a great honor. As many creative individuals do, she suffered from mental illness—she was bipolar. Though not diagnosed properly for decades, she was treated in the late 1940s and 1950s with electroshock treatments to try and help her depression.

My mother, Arleen, wanted two children. She had my sister Nancy when she was twenty-eight years old, but it would take another twelve years for her at thirty-eight to conceive again with me. By that time she had changed as a person and was no longer an ideological young mother. Naturally, she taught me right from wrong and she gave me a strong moral code that she based on trust and honor, but that was where the conventional parenting stopped.

I was four years old and my sister was sixteen when Arleen divorced our father, Jerry, because of his many infidelities. For the first time in her life, at forty-two years of age, she had to find a job to support us, as my father did not pay her the court-ordered child support. She was overwhelmed with the things she needed to learn, even simple things like balancing a checkbook was foreign to her. But she learned quickly and went into the next phase of her life in her unique and unconventional way. Her path was built in part by a wisdom born from her successes and failures and partly by her real understanding of life and what was important and what was not.

She had a definite plan about motherhood for me that no one but her was in favor of. One example was that she never gave me a curfew when I was a teenager. When other parents asked her why, she answered, "I don't have to give her a curfew. If she's going to be bad she doesn't have to wait until 10 pm to be." Her only rule was to let her know where I was and that I was okay. Her expectations of me were high and she held me to it, and I never let her down.

Another example of her thinking was, when I was thirteen and all the other kids at school were sneaking off and hiding in the fields to drink beer, smoke cigarettes, and smoke marijuana, my mother, in her wisdom, decided to bring beer into the house for me. She said if I was determined to do it then at least it was safer this way because I was safe in the house where she could see me. It was the same with marijuana. She didn't buy it, but she let me try it in the house. One of the best memories of my life was watching my mother sitting at the dining room table with my best friend and me drinking peach schnapps and smoking a joint with us. She turned her wig backwards and started laughing like I'd never seen her do before, because she had gotten stoned and in those moments she was joyous and free. But the truth is I soon lost interest in marijuana, probably because I could do it, so the mystique was gone from it and I never smoked it again. My mother's way paid off.

She had a special wisdom and was able to impart so many life lessons that gave me an internal fortitude which I have used my whole life. As an example, when I was struggling to succeed in work and school at the same time, she sat me down and said, "Honey, there are many talented derelicts lying in the gutter. The only difference between the ones who die there and the ones who make it out and succeed is perseverance. Never, never give up on your dreams."

Another example she taught me that made an indelible impression, when life had gotten very hard for a while, was when she explained her way of dealing with hardship. She said, "When life has beaten you down, do what the smart prize fighters do. They go down on one knee and let the referee count them down

1,2,3,4; they stay down until the count of 9, resting, rethinking, gathering courage, and then at the very last second they spring up and kick some ass . . . that's the way to win."

During the times she was depressed, she often stayed in bed for days at a time, watching TV and eating candy or cake. She always ordered take-out food to make sure I was fed, but we would eat it picnic-style in bed watching the sitcoms. Some of those times were the best because she talked to me as if I was an adult, and we bonded as the best of friends in her craziest moments. So I became an avid watcher of As the World Turns and The Young and the Restless just to be with her. Oddly, it was fun to be with her even then. She had a way of pulling me into the ride she was on, and somehow I didn't mind.

When she was manic it would not be unusual for her to take a series of dance lessons at the Arthur Murray dance school and have a torrid affair with a hot young Latin instructor. Or, another favorite was to check into one of the finest hotels on Miami Beach and rent a suite for us to stay in. We ordered in room service, and we would watch pay-per-view movies and, of course, have massages in the room. She loved luxury and experiencing it even in these little getaways from real life weekends. I must admit I have taken on the habit of checking into a luxury hotel and having a spa weekend. It feels wonderful; she was smart for herself even then.

Nancy had married and moved to her own home when I was nine, leaving my mother and me alone. Nancy was more conservative in her thought processes of our mother's parenting skills. She tried to be a stabilizing influence and brought sanity to my life when our mother went into her unpredictable phases, going off on her own for a few days or away with a man she was involved with. Mom called the three of us the Klass women, bonded forever.

All the while she wrote. Writing was her savior. She read her poetry to me at night, and I tried to grasp its depth. As I got older, her poems helped me understand life, its highs and lows, and most of all how to survive. She had many of her poems published in various newspapers and magazines. She wrote under the pseudonym Pan Anderson, as she was able to write more freely being anonymous. She appeared on the "Larry King Show" reading some of her poetry.

In her early seventies, when Arleen was in a retirement home, she met a poor Irish Catholic man, Joe, who used a walker, had vocal surgery, and could hardly speak. She fell madly in love with him and insisted on getting married in the nursing home. When I reminded her she had told us over and over to marry a rich Jewish doctor and that she was doing the opposite, she said, "Don't you worry, do as I say and not as I do." I replied, "Well, he doesn't walk too good and he can hardly speak. What are you so enamored about?" She said, "Never mind all of that, honey, he does other things just fine!" And that was my mother until the end.

Arleen was a survivor and never gave up on love or life or her dreams. She married Joe in a ceremony in the retirement home. They were happily married for three years until he passed away. She lived another six years, enjoying her children and granddaughter Lori, and died peacefully at eighty-two surrounded by her family.

Arleen finished her book of poetry in 1985. She submitted it for publishing, but poetry was not a huge moneymaker and the publishing houses that agreed to publish it wanted the writer to pay half the cost of the first printing. I was a young police officer at the time and didn't have the resources to get the book published. But I promised her that I would one day publish her book and bring her words to the world.

After she passed, I placed her manuscript in a cabinet for safekeeping, and life went on. I revisited it every so often and delighted in her words as if reading them for the first time. I knew I had to find a way to finally bring this book to life.

Arleen was raw and irreverent in the moments these poems were written. For those who feel deeply in good times and in bad, this book is for you. For those who suffer with a depressive disorder, this book is for you to give you courage and hope. For those who simply appreciate poetry, this book is also for you.

Now, thirty years later, my promise is fulfilled. Quiet the theater, dim the lights, finally Arleen Watson has arrived front and center on the biggest stage of her life. Settle into your seat, the curtain is raised. Enjoy all that she has left for us to experience.

Welcome to *Splinters of Glass*.

Donna Watson, September 2016

LONELINESS

Advice to the Lonely

Walk carefully, upon the bright, unfeeling world
Slowly and gracefully, so fear will not show
Fear, and the constant ache of loneliness . . .
Make your laughter sharp and clear . . .
Let all your words glide smoothly—
Keep unsaid all that is you
And all you hope to be.

The Rain Barrel

The rain barrel stands
Outside the farm house
Filled to the brim, replete—
It cannot hold another drop
So, I marvel, how like my life
I, too, am filled to the brim
with pain, with people I cannot forget
What more can harm me?
Everyone I loved is gone—
Either by death or separation
When something hurtful happens now
I feel it, but remotely,
Through muffled walls
Pain taught me how to build.

Summer Wind

I came into your life
Like the summer wind
And for a little while
I made young, green things, grow
In the crevices of stones
That lay across your heart.

But the mechanized tractor of your mind
Exuding poison gas of doubts and fears
Rolled over them and over and over
Until only little broken stems were left—

But like the summer wind
I shall come back to you—
When beauty burns in sudden sunlight
And glints across the open sea
You will stop for a moment—
And you will think of me—
I wish you well—I always will
But I am sad for you
For who again will be so childlike
And so willing to try
To make a garden bloom
Where only stones are laid!

The Drought

It has been a long while now
Since I have had a man to love me—
I have forgotten, or almost
How his touch felt on me—
I thought I no longer needed love
But I was wrong—one shrivels up
When not loved or loving
You feel parched clear through
Like land dried up from lack of rain
Now, I parcel out my days
One, being pretty much like the other—
I guess I hope one day he will come
And my drought will be ended.

Pinnacles

Pinnacles are lonely
There is little room for many
At the top—
One gets tired eventually—
There is no ledge
To rest up there—
The path is steep
And full of rocks
And mud, that batter you
When one descends.

TRAVELS

New York

Spring in New York is always new
For we forget till Spring
How lilacs smell, fuscia velvet
Violets, the fresh scent of grass
After April Showers—
Central Park always kind to its young lovers.
Park Avenue which keeps its poise
Broadway's glitter does not tarnish
Greenwhich Village hearth of artists
They come in an endless stream
The young, the old, searching, hoping
New York, beloved Citadel.

New York Again!

Arrogant wench, in your tiered gown
Of glass and stone
I swear, I will have you yet!
I will be no ant
Crawling in the tunnels at your feet
I will assault your highest peaks—
And you will bow your head to me
And smile, and murmur— "yes!"

Nassau

The hot, white sun beat down
And blanched me free of pain...
The turquoise sea was a siren
And I was her lonely lover—
I lay on the sand
And was part of the reef—
Yes, I found heartsease in Nassau
I will go back Bahamas way
Surely, I will return again.

Rocks in the Sun (Nassau)

I love the feel of rocks
Drowsing in the ageless sun
The warm, satiny wrinkled old rocks
The strong and lonely comfort
Of their backs against mine
I love to sit on the rocks in the sun
Which nestle by an ocean's bay
And gaze as far as the eye can reach
And be free to think what thoughts I may
The Captain of the moment and of my soul.

Reunion

That day on our terrace in Rome
We sat sipping our tiny black espressos
Overhead the birds circled peacefully
Calling to each other as was their wont—
Blissfully, I had no premonition
This would be the last time
I would see you—
Lost somewhere in the bright, blue sea
So like the bright blue of your eyes—
Only the plane, a crippled bird
Was found, drifting sadly
Its head buried in the waves . . .
I know this is not the end
How even now you wait for me
My darling, I will hurry.

SCARS OF THE HEART

The Little Scar

A flame that leaped high and bright
Has gone. Only a little scar remains—
Of all that torrid love and fragile beauty
Time, that surgeon with a magic touch
Has been skilled beyond all belief
Only a little scar remains, but there are
Places where I dare not go—
And passions I am afraid to feel
How that little scar can ache
On a fresh spring night like this—
I am suddenly cold and sick
Will it always be like this?
A profile in a crowd
A song we claimed as ours
A chance acquaintance we both knew
And there is pain from the little scar
That still remains.

The House

I will learn how to build
My house of peace—
Slowly, but surely
Like artisans of old
Built their pyramids
Stone by painful stone—
Then at last
I shall live in a house of stone
Which no wind can shake—
And no love can enter.

For Those Who Come

The ageless eyes
In the old fishermen
Down at the docks
Who daily fight the sea
Comfort me now—
They know that pain—triumph
Like the big fish
Live only their moment
But the sea, like life
Remains long afterwards
For those who come.

Birth of Joy

Wonder filled my being
At the birth of this new thing—Joy!
I built no words to house it
Lest the weight of my breath
Frighten it away—
So I stood, mutely—
Clasping this fragile, fledgling—
To my breast.

War

Other women have wept
As you weep now
Apart, in a room alone—
But they have gone on
Their faces cold and smooth
Eyes blank, careful smiles upon their lips
Will you be less brave?
Keen for your man
Lost somewhere in this
Senseless horror we call war
Purge your grief, here in this room
Alone except for Him—
Then emerge, and begin your fight
With smiles and cheerful talk
And wholesome cooking
For the little ones
Shield them, if you can
From your shattered world
For your heroic efforts
After a time, will come peace—
But now there is no balm
To salve the brutal fact
Your man lies dead in Korea.

New Generation

There was no time for us
When we were young
The wars, you know—
And all of that—
Now like broken, dancing dolls
We falter on a string too short,
What of our children now?
Perhaps they will be able
To pick up fragments here and there
And slowly mend and glue,
And make us whole again.

The Little Ones

Do not let them get lonely—
The little ones, growing up . . .
They are young, so little
And old so much. Be there! . . .
I know the worthy causes
Needing help, doing worthy things
The card games, too, keep calling—
And I know your need of fun,
But they are young so little—
Do not let them get lonely.

BITTER HARVEST

Survival

To keep trying is the answer
Even though you walk
Feeling your way—
Not knowing what lies ahead
Stumbling and falling
And crying out
But still walking!
Still hoping the next day
Will be better—
Grateful, when a small ray
Of sunshine falls upon you
For a short time
Grateful for its warmth.

Sick-abed

I lay sick-abed
And did not know which was sicker
My soul or my head—
I looked out my window
And saw the shivering trees
Shaking the brown leaves from their limbs
Waiting out the winter cold
Looking for the Spring to come
And with it new promises . . .
Will there be new hope for me
With the coming of the robin and the rose?

Pain

They say pain lessens with time—
Does it really
Or does it take another form?
Does wild anguish
Eventually turn to numbness?
Is that what they mean
When they say
Time heals all wounds?
But numbness is worse than pain
In pain, there is life
When you feel nothing
It is like dying.

The Puzzle

Somewhere along the way
I got lost—
I stopped trying to win—
I lost that rage to succeed—
You have to burn with wanting it
Be willing to do anything—
Anything at all!
There at last is my answer—
I wanted it easy and nice
Like when I was young
And everything came to me
Without my even asking!
I fold my cards
I do not want to play—
But life does not let you quit
Somehow, you have to go on
Here I am, cadging my bets
Hoping for the best.

The Thirst

There is a hurting, yearning
Inside of me, that will not stop—
Only you, if you would come
Could slake, for a moment
This painful thirst, that drives me so
You would give me wine to drink
A bitter, hot, sweet wine to drink
That for a matchless instant
Would seem to quench my thirst
Refusing to believe it
Will not really make me well
But merely make me thirst once more.

Affair at End

To have it end like this
With just your smile and shrug
Here in this firelit room
With its ocean view—is not decent.
In a room whose walls are dank with slime
And yes, blood rusting on the floor
And chains hanging from my wrists and feet
Pain, so sharp, it stops the heart
Is expected, and can be borne with dignity
But not here, in this firelit room
With its ocean view.

Rhapsody

Music, beloved friend
How I worship you!
You wrap me in your beauty
And I am no longer lonely—
You envelop me
I feel safe and warm
I drift off into some lovely world
Where everyone is loved and loving—
As long as I have the magic of you
The cares, the worries of the day fade
And I am in command of the moment!

The Foolish Heart

"Be still, I coaxed my heart...
Let me rock on my hearth—
It will be winter soon
And I am far from young—
I have had enough of love
And sighing, let me be..."
But here was this dark-eyed stranger
With his vowing and his pleading—
And oh—his smile was fair to see...
I felt the old, sweet madness start
As he and my foolish, child heart
Had me tumbled fast out the door
I ran, half laughing, half crying—
For I was far from young
And knew the end
Before the game had half begun!

To a Woman Very Dear

Ah, my sister—
You are afraid for me,
I feel your tears upon my hand,
Oh, my dear, I tell you this—
He will come back one day!
One cannot hope to nest an eagle
All at once. Let him fly free!
Let him know the cold, vast skies,
Even an eagle tires.
He will return—
But I tell you this, my dear—
If he never comes again, I still rejoice
That once he loved me a little
And I will walk this quiet valley
With head held proudly high,
For to be loved by an eagle,
Even for a little, is no small thing.

THE FAMILY

Donna – Flight

She is gone from me
Except in my thoughts
I see her laughing, teasing me
Full of love—
Not spoken always, but there
For me to know and feel,
I am left now
With only echoes of her,
"Keep busy" well meaning friends say
So, I am busy the livelong day—
There is the job, chores,
Neighbor's chatter, the soap operas
But all the while
My heart is still, so still
Like the trussed up bird
In the knapsack of the
Hunter at day's end.

Donna – The Road

Storm child of my heart
Whom I must love
Till the moment I die—
Go onward and upward
On the roads you will choose
We do not know
What lies ahead
Behind each hardly opened gate
But I can hope
That in the years
That you belonged to me alone
I made you wise and unafraid.

The Little Brown Seal
(Donna)

Little brown seal
Come play with me
So sleek and smooth
You rollover and over
And flirt with me
You watch me between your paws
You take a gleeful jump into the air
Then you paddle away
Then you come back
And look at me
Your head cocked to one side
"Catch me if you can"
You seem to say
"I like you, but I cannot stay"
I pretend not to care
But I do care and hope
You will come back
I will always watch for you.

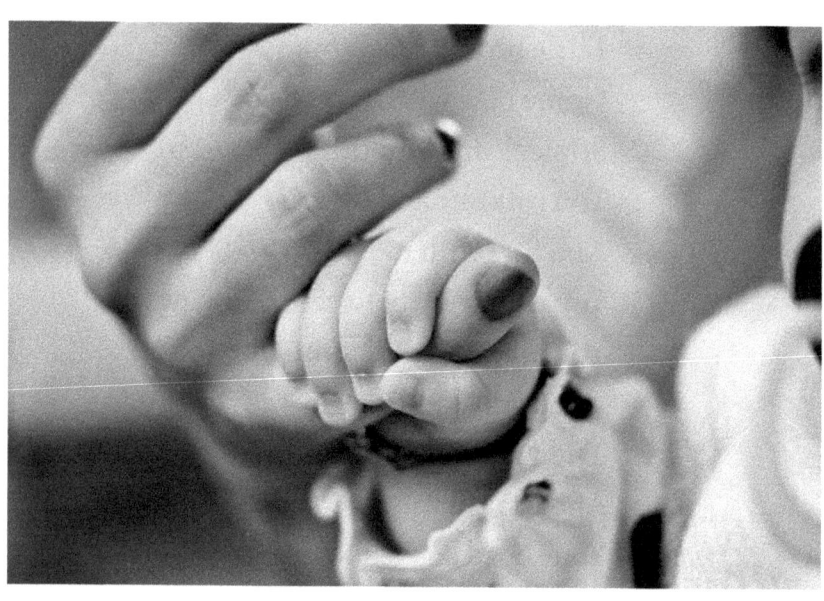

Nancy

I was always able to love you in joy
Even as a child there was a serenity
About you that made me feel safe and calm
Your great blue eyes looking up at me
So steadfastly, your hand holding mine
In perfect trust
You have always been
A living statement of your love.

My Sister – The Visit

My loved one has gone away—
But not beyond recall
Memories of happy times with her
Come flooding back
Like morning sunlight
Streaming through the dining room windows
As we chatted and ate
Huge mounds of Sunday brunch
Now, we are at the beach
Tying up our hair
Before that first icy plunge
Into the sparkling waves—
Now, we are climbing the cliff
Pausing only to rest
To look far out to sea—
The warm comfort of the satiny rocks
Against our backs as we sit a moment
Those days will not come again
But she lives always in my heart
And we visit often.

Mother

If only I could have known you—
But you died when I was small
How it must have distressed you to leave me
All I have of you
Is a faded color miniature
Done in the fashion of your day
High pompador sweeping back
From a regal brow
Deep set eyes, serene lips
The heavy, gold chain and watch
You wore around your neck
My knowledge of you comes from stories
My sisters would tell me—
I never tired of hearing them
They would tell me of your calm—
Your strength, your kindness to all—
You were the keeper of the peace
Whenever there was a quarrel
You would put your finger to your lips
And softly say "Hush"—
Suddenly, whatever storm had been
Was over, and all were friends again
How many times I have cried out
To your painted miniature
"Oh, Mother, if only I could
Put my head on your breast"
Your calm eyes stare back at me
I hear you softly say "Hush"—
Suddenly, things seem better.

My Husband

I watched you
Walk through the orchard
The trees bent down to you,
Heavy with their sweet burden
You looked neither to the left or right
The sun found your face
You did not raise your head
You walked on—
Lost in some private world
Where no one but you may enter
What strange man is this
Who is my husband?
You are alone
Like a mountain is alone
Proud, needing no one—
Thoughts of you come unbidden
Like cold, sweet water
Bubbling, secret underground—
I stay a willing captive—
To my love for you.

PEBBLES

The Doe

Beauty born afresh
That is you!
Rapture captured! That is you.
Then what is wrong?
What is it I almost see?
You are so lovely one is afraid to look—
Lest they be blinded by your radiance
Is it that your smile
Is like winter sun on ice
Bright without warmth?
Is it that I have seen you
Tread on flowers without noticing
Is it that I have seen your look before
In the sleek doe—
Who at the water's edge
Will turn to stare at you
With her great souless eyes.

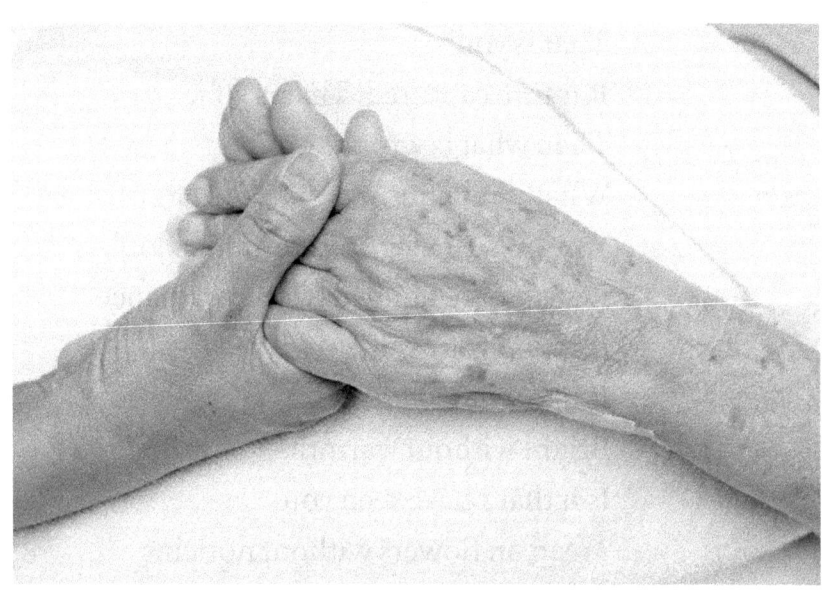

Death Dances Too

So now you finally have come—
And I have met you face to face—
Do I seem afraid? I am not.
Tell me when and I shall get my coat
The dance is done, the hour late
I will not be sorry to leave
I have even watched the door
Hoping you would come fetch me—
So what now? Shall I bid them all adieu?
No. Let us just leave quietly . . .
I have had so much of shrill laughter
And noisy, insincere farewells—
Let us go quietly
I shall be glad to go
As I am tired.

The Loner

I think I was born lonely—
There was a distance between
Me and the rest of the world
I could never seem to bridge
There was no warmth for me
At anyone's fire
I would watch people's faces
Looking for the sign—
The "yes" I want you look
Somehow, except for brief encounters
They would go their way
Leaving me more lonely than before.

Thoughts

Like gossamer wings
Of humming birds
Thoughts of yesterdays
Enter my mind softly
Persistently, but gently
I see the green years
Go by me
In so short a time—
The bitter sweet spring
Of my youth—
Love came shyly by
And then ran away
I never knew why—
Summer blossoming came slowly—
But I had my harvest moon
And a dark, lean lover
To sing me a silvery tune—
Suddenly, or so it seemed

Winter came, and there
Was snow and cold everywhere
No matter how hard
I pounded up the grate
The fire never seemed to warm me
I took to wearing shawls
And put my hair up in a bun
Now I poke the fire
And put the kettle on for tea
And wonder how many years are left for me
To sit and sigh
And remember times
That will not come again.

The Shopper

You cannot buy love
Although you shop for it all your life
You can go into a pastry shoppe
And buy fresh baked buns and bread
But nowhere is that magic shoppe
That stocks happiness or peace
So you stand forlornly
Clutching your dollar bills
Knowing in your heart
That what you seek so earnestly
Is given freely or not at all.

The Summit

I climb upward
To the cliff's summit
Blue skies and white clouds flying
The soaring birds make little calling sounds
As they swoop and dip overhead
I feel elated!
Powerful, and yet at peace,
My soul passes from me
And flies upward to the sun
I do not know where I am going—
I only know where I have been
And that I do not want
To stay there anymore . . .

MEMORIES

Memories

I do not want to leave my memories
Of people I have known and loved
They are more real to me
Than anything that happens now
The sweet glamour of days gone by
Old cities I have been part of
Where their beauty was so great
It made my heart ache
For we are the spoilers
We cannot leave anything alone
Wherever I went
Every man had a smile for me
When one has had the homage of a queen
It is hard to live without it.

In Memory

She was not a learned woman
As the world judges these things
To me, she was wise and kind and gay
She is gone now and we who knew her mourn
Perhaps God thought "You had her for awhile
Now, I need her up here with me!"

The Party

We gave a party
You and I
And Love came to our feast
Love, in a soiled gown with bare feet...
Joy came, but did not stay
Honor did not come at all
And Truth came at the end...
But Love was there
In a soiled gown
With bare feet.

Blue Midnight

The night has me by the throat
As the twilight starts to darken
I feel the panic begin—
Suddenly the night is all around me
Like the big, black cat he is—
I try to reason with myself
"See," I say, "there is nothing here"
Suddenly, a quick movement
Or so it seems—
A shadow in the hall
Paralyzes me with fright
I wait. Nothing happens.
I force myself to get up.
Everything is fine.
The mirrors look down at me pityingly
The radio plays on. Love songs—
All about unrequited love
Boy, I could tell them!
I look at the clock—
Only three more hours til dawn
The coming of the light releases me!

The Outsider

I marvel that no one notices
I daily move among them
And am accepted
I do my given tasks
I work, I talk, I laugh —
And no one knows
I watch them from my vantage point
And with great caring wonder
At their stupidities —
How they waste their time
They think they have forever
Or perhaps, they do not think at all
They crowd into the marketplace
Hawking their wares
I am no part of them
They have nothing I want
But I hope all goes well with them.

THE MEN

Al Jolson

The throat of song burst
The tired, valiant heart
Which really has not died
You live as you have always
In the hearts of those to whom
Music of all kinds is a shrine
You are not gone far away
You will live always in our hearts.

I Am So Free

I am so free
Now that my heart broke
There are so many things to do
Cupboards to be straightened
Silver to be polished
Letters that need answering
Things like that to do
Now that you are gone
No need to cook supper
Just for me—
No need to buy flowers
And fashion them just so
No need to watch the clock
Every hour will be the same
Tick tock, tick tock,
But no you coming in the door
Maybe I will get used to it—
They say you can get used to anything.

My Doctor

With your first quizzical glance
I knew you would save me
But what were your thoughts
As you looked at this mangled,
bloody piece of flesh?
Could you save her? Should you?
This is all I remember for awhile
Then your hypnotic soothing voice
Spreading your healing balm
Over the worst places of me
Then life giving rivulets
Begin to join others
And soon I begin to want to live again.

Dr. Jack Greener

We have so many silent conversations
Interspersed with our verbal ones
"How are you today?" you will ask
Then your silent communication adds
"I'm really glad to see you."

"I am very well today," I will answer
But my heart adds, "I am so happy to see you,"
A tiny drop of honey is what you give me
Each time we meet
A tiny drop of honey steeped in the wine
Of your wisdom and compassion

But do you really know how tired I am?
The road back seems endless
Still, if you are willing to try
So must I, for so many reasons.

Piper Pan

Piper Pan, Piper Pan, how do I pay you
For this lovely tune you play me on your pipe?
Will it be in golden coin, or silver spangles
Shining bright?
Piper Pan, Piper Pan where will you lead me?
All around a country lane.
Will you bring me back again?
Safe and sound? Safe and sound?
Piper Pan! Piper Pan!
Shall I wear my pretty gown?
Will he take me into town?
Will I meet a Fairy Prince?
Will he find me very fair, Piper Pan, Piper Pan?
Will his love be ever true, Piper Pan, Piper Pan?
Lead me gaily, lead me true, but promise me
I can return with you!

About the Author

Arleen Klass Watson was born August 27, 1922, in Ohio. Her mother died shortly after her birth, and she was taken to New York City to be raised by her sisters. She was the youngest of six brothers and sisters. Two of her siblings died at young ages. The loss of her mother had a profound effect on Arleen throughout her life, and it influenced her writing.

Arleen fell in love with the New York stage and attended the American Academy of Dramatic Arts and performed in many Off Broadway plays. Her roommate was Lauren Bacall. Her love of acting, dancing, and writing began there. She fell in love and married just before WWII began. He was a lieutenant in the army, and she was forced to leave New York to live on several military bases he was stationed at, leaving behind her dreams of acting and stardom. It was not a happy marriage. They did have two children, both daughters twelve years apart. In 1964, Arleen found the courage to divorce him and begin her life anew.

She made her home in Miami, Florida. She raised her children and began a career in her late forties in public relations for a South Beach hospital where she entertained local socialites. She fell in love again years later with an older man who was twenty-five years her senior. He was a married man, and though he would not leave his wife, he was the true love of Arleen's life. Their secret affair began in a bungalow by the beach and lasted many years, until he passed away.

Arleen's life motto was Never Give Up, and she never did. In the last years of her lifetime, after decades of emotional unrest, she found peace in her heart and in her mind. The wisdom of aging and the acceptance of her fate led her to finding God on her own terms, which is how she lived each day of her life.

Splinters of Glass is the expression of a complex woman and the promise fulfilled of a loving daughter. Arleen Watson suffered from severe lows and euphoric highs in her life, but was still able to conquer the obstacles that stood in her way with an internal strength and deep wisdom. Born decades too early for her way she moved in the world, suffering painful losses and a lifelong battle with depression, she was still able to love and squeeze the last drop out of life. The deeply passionate way she viewed the world is expressed in the darkness and light of her poetry. I highly recommend this work of art as an expression of the beauty that cannot be limited by mental illness, but serves to overcome it.

George Kallas, Psy.D., Ph.D.

All proceeds of the book sales will be donated to:

Dr. Donna's Pet Foundation

My mother always loved animals, in particular dogs and cats. I would watch her face come alive when she watched them play. She connected with them in a place of peace and they brought her such joy. She knew she could trust their love. I know she would be so happy and so proud that she could play a part in giving abandoned animals a chance at happiness and refuge from the cold reality of being helpless to fend for themselves. So all of the proceeds from her book sales will be donated to our cause.

Dr. Donna's Pet Foundation

Is a 501(c)(3) foundation with the sole purpose of raising funds to help homeless, abused, and in need pets, and pet rescue organizations within our tri-county area.

Our mission is to save as many animals from high-kill shelters and horrible living conditions that many find themselves in either by neglect, abandonment, natural disasters, or over population in a small vicinity such as in hoarding houses or unscrupulous breeders.

Our foundation is a completely volunteer organization with all of the profits going to the causes of animals that have no voice to help themselves. Your donations will be spent responsibly. All donations will go to further the mission of this foundation. Nothing will be wasted or used for any other endeavor or to pay salaries of board members.

Achieving a time where there are no homeless pets is Dr. Donna's Pet Foundation's mission. We are working with humane groups all across the tri-county area to bring about a time when homeless, abandoned animals are no longer being destroyed in shelters and mistreated within our communities.

Dr. Donna's Pet Foundation is an organization committed to saving the lives of homeless pets through effective adoption and spay-neuter programs, leading the way to changing legislation, and to champion for stronger laws and enforcement of those laws for abusers of animal rights.

"No pet should be without a home, and no human heart should be without the unconditional love that having one brings."

www.ingramcontent.com/pod-product-compliance
Lightning Source LLC
Chambersburg PA
CBHW070502100426
42743CB00010B/1732